Note Reading Made FUN

Note Reading, Book 1

Kevin and Julia Olson

Production: Frank J. Hackinson
Production Coordinators: Peggy Gallagher and Philip Groeber
Editors: Edwin McLean and Peggy Gallagher
Cover and Interior Illustrations: Julia Olson
Engraving: Tempo Music Press, Inc.
Printer: Tempo Music Press, Inc.

ISBN-13: 978-1-56939-943-9

Table of Contents

Notes to the Teacher and Parent . . .

Piano Made FUN for the Young® is an early childhood piano curriculum designed to teach and reinforce the basics of piano study, in a spirit of FUN, PLAYFULNESS, and SUCCESS. The curriculum consists of *Sing-Along Activity Books* and leveled piano books with complimentary audio recordings. Notes and concepts are taught at a careful and steady pace, giving students a solid foundation without moving too quickly. It is especially effective in a group setting, but great for private students as well.

Young children enjoy lessons that offer a variety of experiences. This curriculum provides diverse learning opportunities that incorporate singing, movement, games, and more. A typical lesson is divided into two areas:

 *Theory Made FUN; Counting Made FUN; Notes Made FUN*

During Rug Time, students sit on the floor near the piano and sing songs using the *Sing-Along Activity Books* to learn and review concepts. Singing the simple songs keeps their attention and helps them have fun while learning. Teachers who are not comfortable singing can use the recordings to listen to the songs with their students. Because the songs are short and easy to remember, many of them can be reviewed in a matter of minutes. **The beginning of each unit in the piano books indicates which concepts to cover at Rug Time.**

Piano Time *Pre-Reading Made FUN, Starter Book; Note Reading Made FUN, Book 1*

During Piano Time, students use the leveled piano books with recordings to learn to play and read music at a pace that is steady and comfortable. The music is simple and easy to read so young students do not become frustrated. The themed units and play-along recordings make the learning process fun and interesting. (Each piece is recorded at a slow practice tempo; students may follow the indicated tempo and dynamic when ready.)

This *Note Reading Made FUN, Book 1* is the second piano book used during Piano Time. It teaches and reinforces the notes in Middle C hand position. New notes are introduced at a steady and comfortable pace, with plenty of reinforcement. Each unit uses an animal theme—such as cats, dogs, and elephants—to correlate with the new note introduced.

We are confident this curriculum will give young students an effective way to get started with the piano, in an atmosphere they can enjoy!

Remember, you can visit **www.PianoMadeFun.com** for free printables and teaching aids.

Kevin and Julia Olson

Practice Time at Home . . .

It is very important for parents to be willing to participate with daily practice time at home. You do not need to spend *much* time, but it is important to spend *some* time each day. Young students need careful supervision when they are first learning new pieces.

Here are a few suggestions for practice time at home:

Start out each practice session with a few songs from the *Sing-Along Activity Books.* (You may wish to use the recordings.) Check to see which unit your child's teacher has assigned for the week, and look at the beginning of that unit to find which songs to sing. You do not need to sing every song every day. Try to sing each song at least a few times per week, so your child can become familiar with the concepts. Young children enjoy singing the same songs over and over.

Once you have finished singing a few of the songs, move to the piano to help your child practice the pieces the teacher has assigned in *Note Reading Made FUN, Book 1.* Listen to the recording first, then help your child practice without the recording until they are ready to play with it. Encourage your child to practice each piece slowly and carefully, with nicely curved fingers. You may want to point along in the music as your child practices a new piece. Once he/she is comfortable, you won't need to point any longer.

Remember that young children need consistent reinforcement. You may even find that they sometimes forget something they have already learned. This is normal. Be patient and consistent and your child will eventually learn the pieces. It is also a good idea to consistently review old pieces. Just because your child has moved ahead in the book, does not mean he/she should stop playing the pieces already learned. This is a good time for your child to play the pieces along with the recordings. Young children love to play pieces that are comfortable to them, so go back and review pieces often.

Visit **www.PianoMadeFun.com** for more detailed instructions on how to help your child practice the pieces in this book. You can also go there for supplemental games and activities to do with your child at home.

Teacher Information for Rug Time . . .

The pictures below represent the concepts that will be covered during Rug Time using the *Sing-Along Activity Books.* They are listed here for easy reference. It is not meant for students to memorize all of these concepts at once. Students will memorize and retain the information as they sing the songs and review them each week. The beginning of each unit will indicate which concepts to cover for that unit. Visit **www.PianoMadeFun.com** for resources to use at Rug Time.

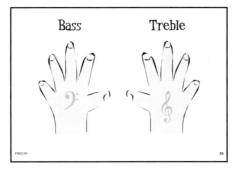
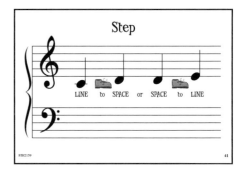

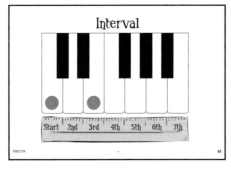

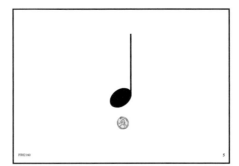
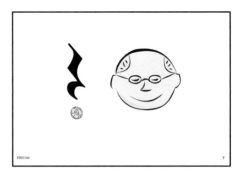

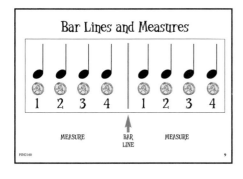
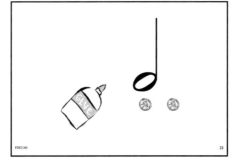
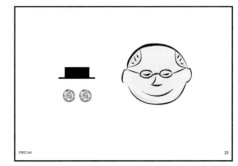

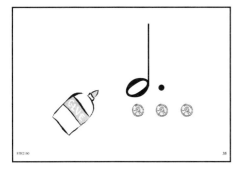

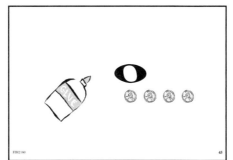

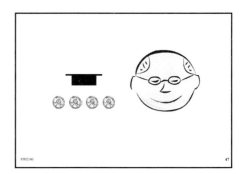

Middle C Hand Position . . .

The notes in this book are in Middle C position. To play in Middle C position, place both thumbs on the C that is in the middle of the piano. Place the rest of your fingers as indicated in the note guide below. We will give each of the notes an animal name for fun.

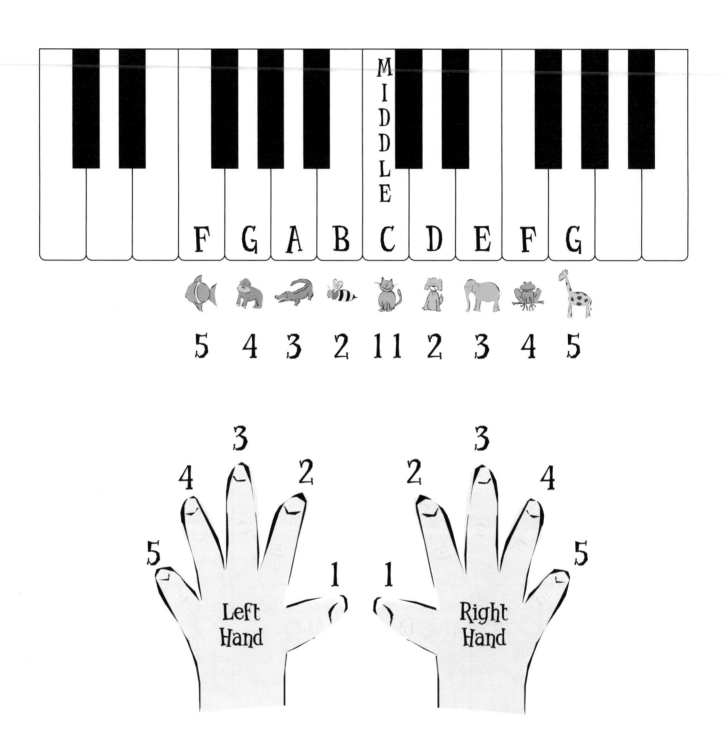

Hand positions are only "guides." They help you feel comfortable learning new notes. Once you are comfortable, your   teacher will help you explore your pieces further by starting on a different finger.

FJH21

Getting Comfortable in Middle C Position . . .

Practice playing the notes in Middle C position. With one hand at a time, place your fingers in position, then play each note going up, then going down as shown with the animal pictures below. The finger numbers are there to guide you. You can play this as a warm-up every day for practice time at home.

Right Hand

Left Hand

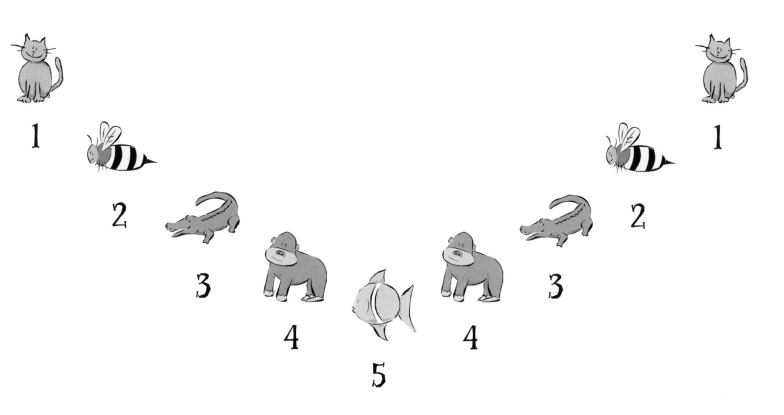

UNIT 1

Rug Time

Theory Made FUN Sing-Along Book tracks 1, 15-20.
Counting Made FUN Sing-Along Book tracks 1-8.
Notes Made FUN Sing-Along Book tracks 1-2.

Piano Time

Cat Note C

CAT NOTE C ON THE KEYBOARD:

Find and play all of the C's on your piano. Now find the C that is in the middle of your piano. It is called Middle C, but we will call it Cat Note C for fun. You can play Cat Note C with R.H. finger 1.

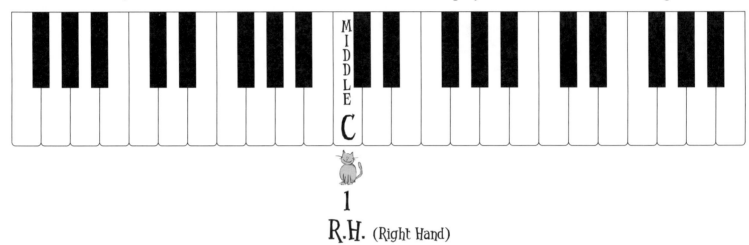

R.H. (Right Hand)

CAT NOTE C ON THE STAFF:

Cat Note C floats below the treble staff, with a little line through the middle of it.

Repeat Sign

Play the example below, keeping your eyes on the music.

1st time: Name notes and play.
2nd time: Count and play.

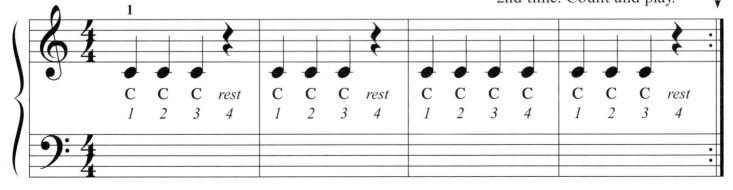

After you are comfortable with this piece, try playing Cat Note C with **R.H.** finger **2**.

Dog Note D

DOG NOTE D ON THE KEYBOARD:
Find and play all of the D's on your piano. Now find the D that is above Cat Note C.
We will call it Dog Note D for fun. You can play Dog Note D with R.H. finger 2.

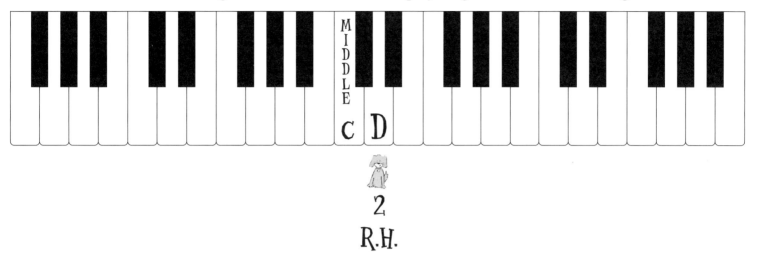

DOG NOTE D ON THE STAFF:
Dog Note D sits on the space just below the treble staff, touching the bottom line.

Play the example below, keeping your eyes on the music.　　1st time: Name notes and play.
2nd time: Count and play.

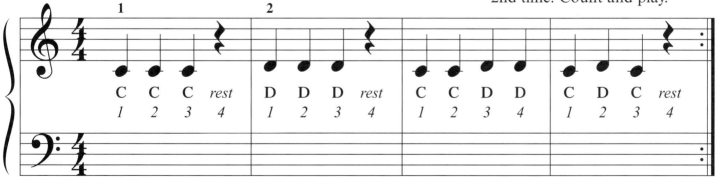

After you are comfortable with this piece, try playing Cat Note C with **R.H.** finger **2**.

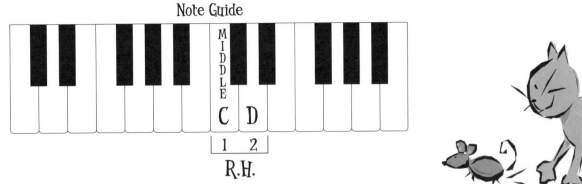

Note Guide

MIDDLE
C D
1 2
R.H.

Mouse Should Hide 1

Cat Note C to Dog Note D is an interval of a second, or a step.

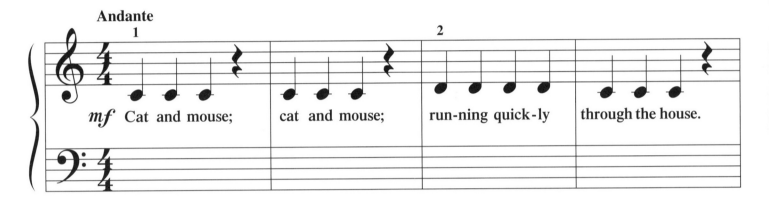

Andante

mf Cat and mouse; cat and mouse; run-ning quick-ly through the house.

Mouse should hide ver - y fast, then he would be safe at last.

Teacher Duet: Student plays as written.

mp

FJH216

Note Guide

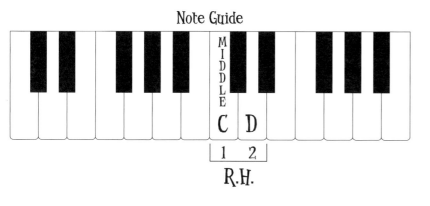

Dog is Chasing Cat 2

Allegro

mf Now the dog is | chas - ing cat. | Now the dog is | chas - ing cat.

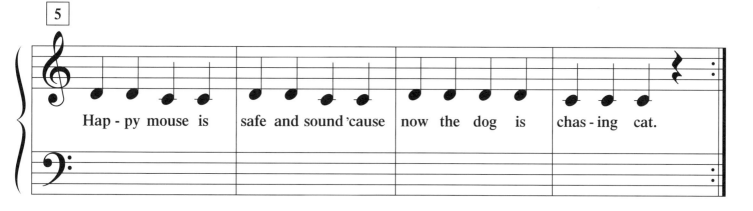

5

Hap - py mouse is | safe and sound 'cause | now the dog is | chas - ing cat.

Teacher Duet: Student plays as written.

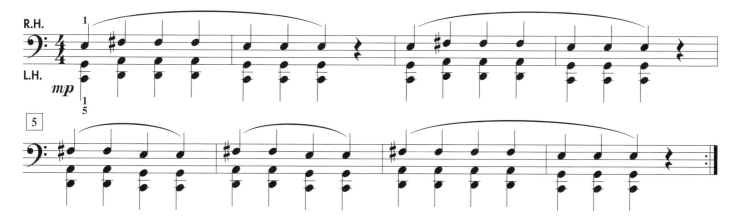

R.H.

L.H. mp

5

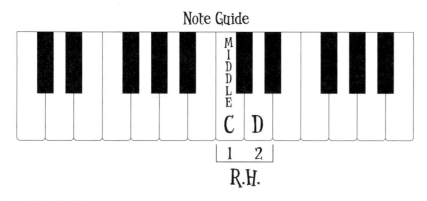

Note Guide

Running Through the Park ③

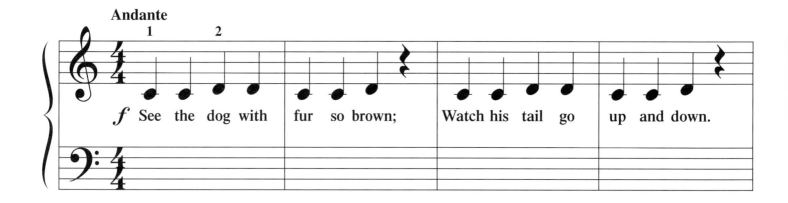

Andante

f See the dog with | fur so brown; | Watch his tail go | up and down.

5 See the dog and | hear him bark; | Watch him run-ning | through the park.

Teacher Duet: Student plays as written.

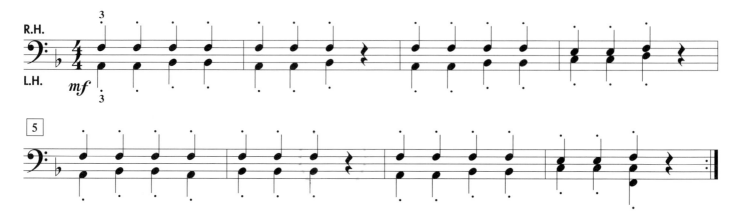

R.H.

L.H. *mf*

FJH216

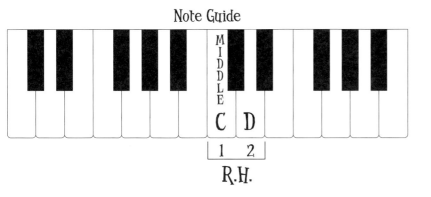

Note Guide

Tasty, Crunchy Bone 4

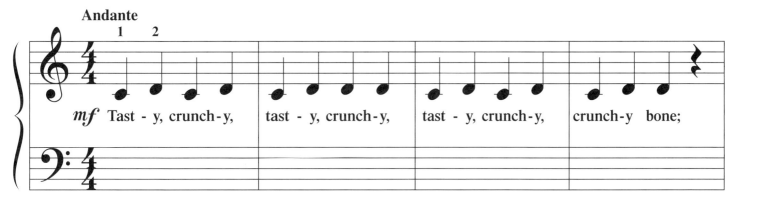

Andante

mf Tast - y, crunch-y, tast - y, crunch-y, tast - y, crunch-y, crunch-y bone;

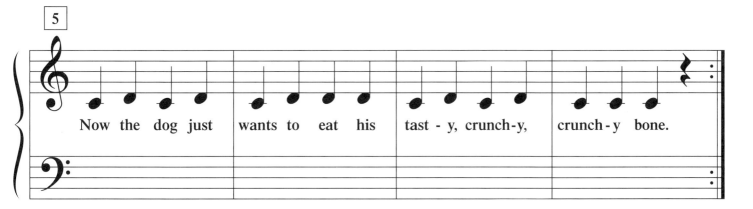

5

Now the dog just wants to eat his tast - y, crunch-y, crunch-y bone.

Teacher Duet: Student plays as written.

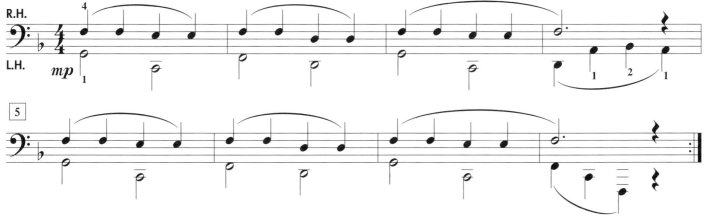

Theory Made FUN Sing-Along Book tracks 1, 15-20.
Counting Made FUN Sing-Along Book tracks 9-15.
Notes Made FUN Sing-Along Book tracks 1-3.

Elephant E

ELEPHANT E ON THE KEYBOARD:

Find and play all of the E's on your piano. Now find the E that is above Dog Note D.
We will call it Elephant E for fun. You can play Elephant E with R.H. finger 3.

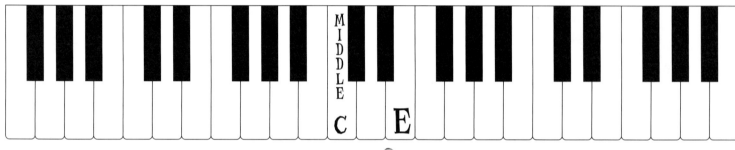

ELEPHANT E ON THE STAFF:

Elephant E sits on line number 1 of the treble staff.

Play the example below, keeping your eyes on the music.

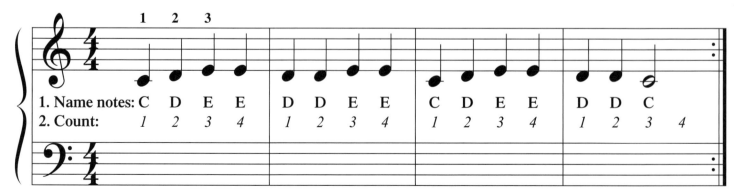

	1	2	3												
1. Name notes:	C	D	E	E	D	D	E	E	C	D	E	E	D	D	C
2. Count:	1	2	3	4	1	2	3	4	1	2	3	4	1	2	3	4

After you are comfortable with this piece, try playing Cat Note C with **R.H.** finger **2**.

FJH2161

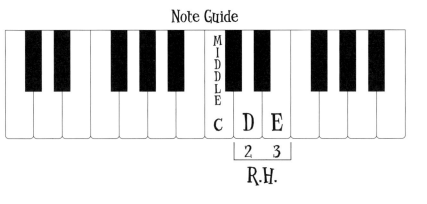

Note Guide

Elephant Ride 5

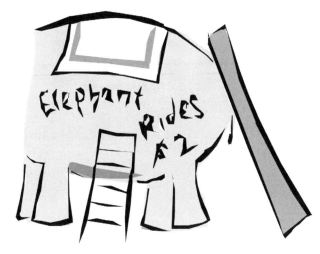

Largo

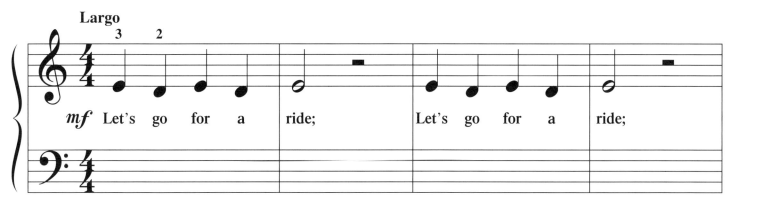

mf Let's go for a ride; Let's go for a ride;

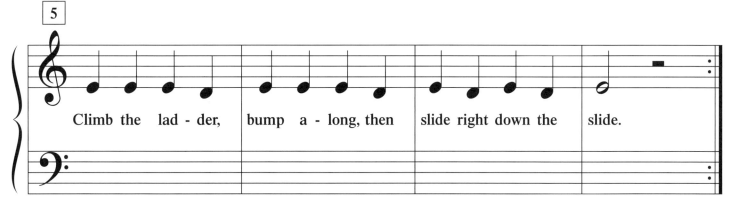

Climb the lad - der, bump a - long, then slide right down the slide.

Teacher Duet: Student plays as written.

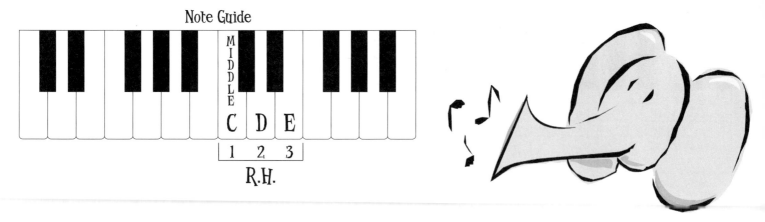

Note Guide

Like a Trumpet 6

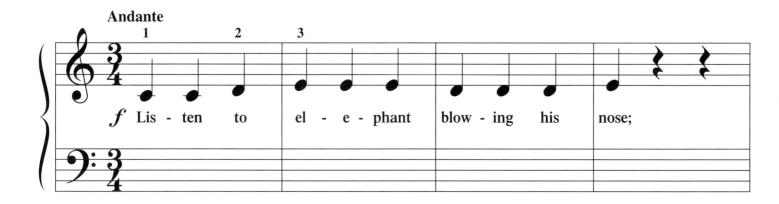

Andante

f Lis - ten to el - e - phant blow - ing his nose;

Sounds like a trum - pet wher - ev - er he goes.

Teacher Duet: Student plays as written.

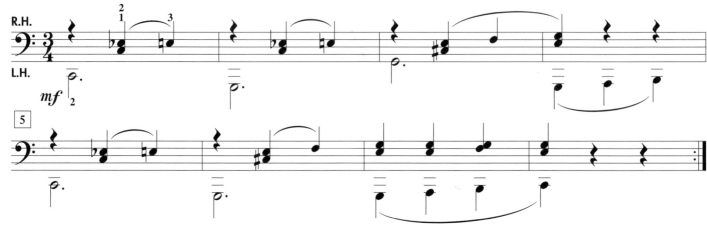

18

FJH21

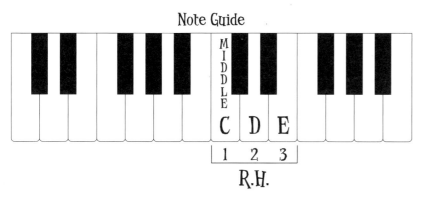

Elephant Will Not Forget ⑦

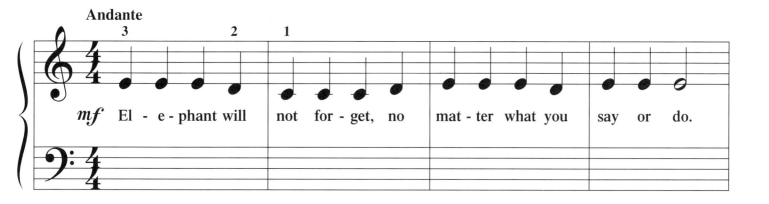

Andante

mf El - e - phant will | not for - get, no | mat - ter what you | say or do.

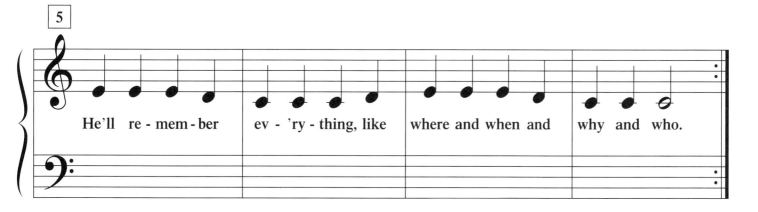

He'll re - mem - ber | ev - 'ry - thing, like | where and when and | why and who.

Teacher Duet: Student plays as written.

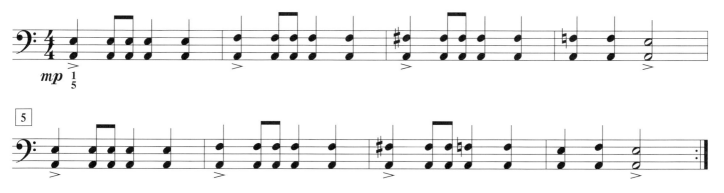

mp

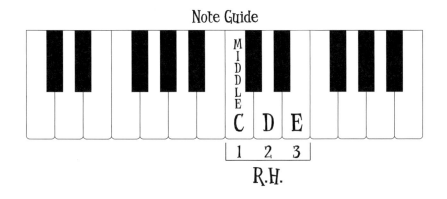

Salty Popcorn 8

Andante

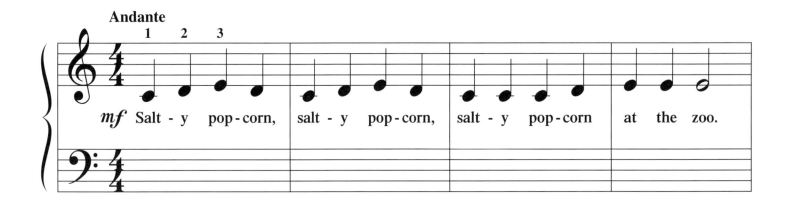

mf Salt - y pop-corn, salt - y pop-corn, salt - y pop-corn at the zoo.

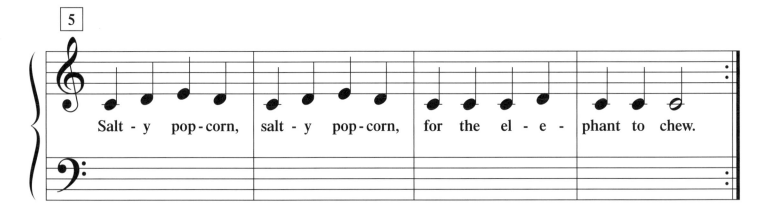

Salt - y pop-corn, salt - y pop-corn, for the el - e - phant to chew.

Teacher Duet: Student plays as written.

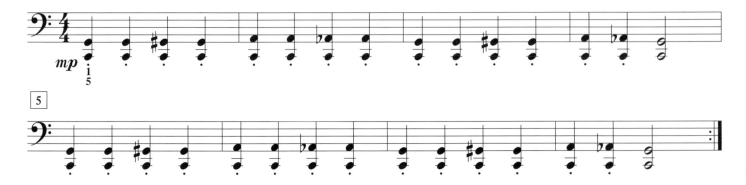

FJH216

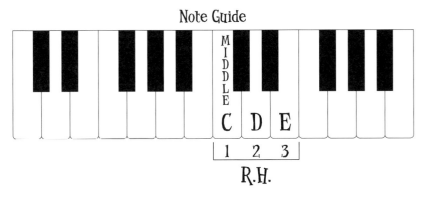

Note Guide

Leathery Gray 9

Cat Note C to Elephant Note E is an interval of a third, or a skip.

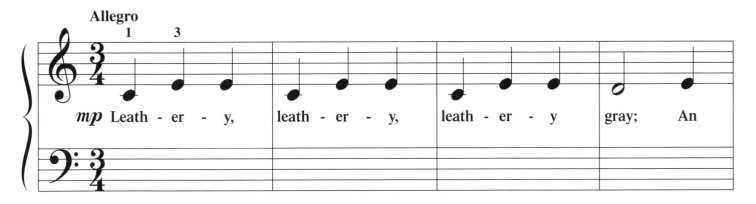

Allegro

mp Leath - er - y, leath - er - y, leath - er - y gray; An

el - e - phant's skin looks so leath - er - y gray.

Teacher Duet: Student plays as written.

UNIT 3

Rug Time

Theory Made FUN Sing-Along Book tracks 1, 15-20.
Counting Made FUN Sing-Along Book tracks 16-20.
Notes Made FUN Sing-Along Book tracks 1-3, 13-14.

Piano Time

Cat Note C

Review CAT NOTE C ON THE KEYBOARD:
Find and play Cat Note C on the keyboard. This time, play it with L.H. finger 1.

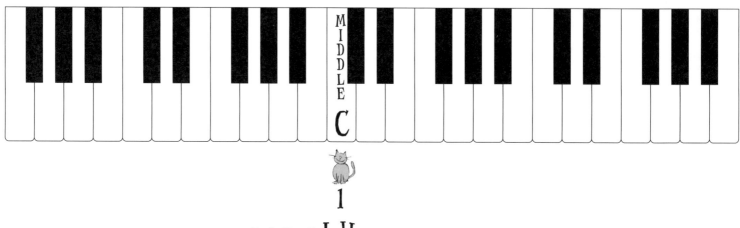

(Left Hand) **L.H.**

CAT NOTE C ON THE STAFF:
Cat Note C can also sit near the bass staff with its stem going down.

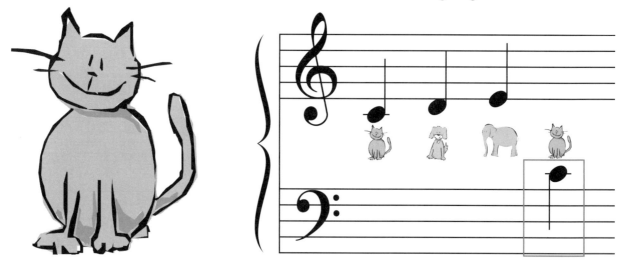

Place both hands on the piano to play the example below, keeping your eyes on the music.
Sing the words and play.

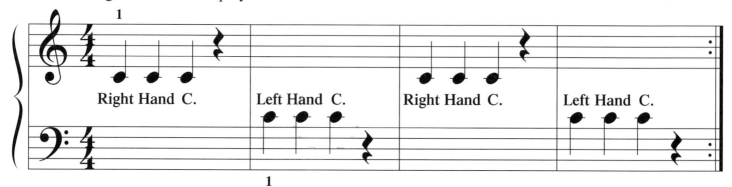

Right Hand C.   Left Hand C.   Right Hand C.   Left Hand C.

FJH2163

Bee Note B

BEE NOTE B ON THE KEYBOARD:
Find and play all of the B's on your piano. Now find the B that is below Cat Note C.
We will call it Bee Note B for fun. You can play Bee Note B with L.H. finger 2.

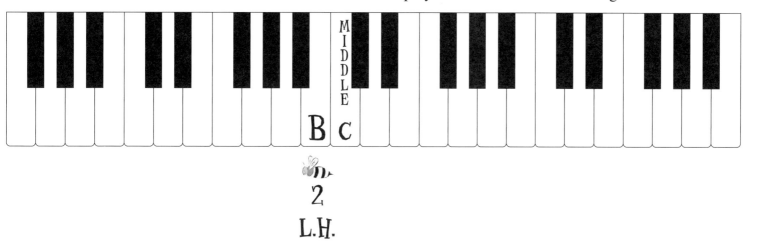

BEE NOTE B ON THE STAFF:
Bee Note B sits on the space just above the bass staff.

Play the example below, keeping your eyes on the music.

| 1. Name notes: | C | B | C | B | C | C | C | C | B | B | B | B | C | | | |
| 2. Count: | 1 | 2 | 3 | 4 | 1 | 2 | 3 | 4 | 1 | 2 | 3 | 4 | 1 | 2 | 3 | 4 |

After you are comfortable with this piece, try playing Cat Note C with **L.H.** finger **2**.

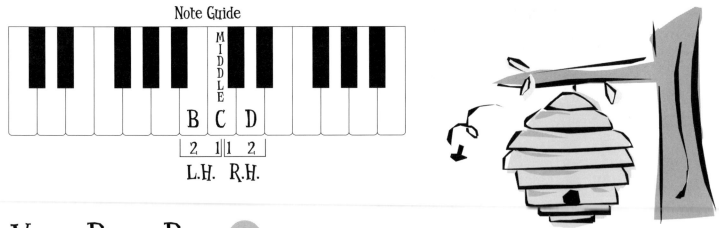

Note Guide

Very Busy Bee 10

Cat Note C to Bee Note B is an interval of a second.

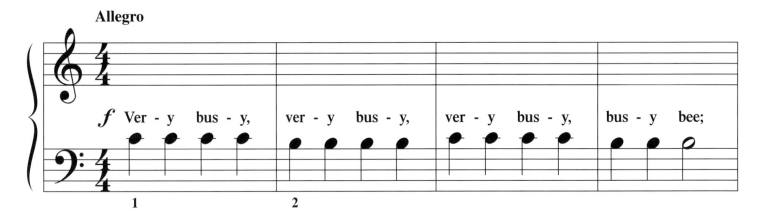

Allegro

f Ver - y bus - y, ver - y bus - y, ver - y bus - y, bus - y bee;

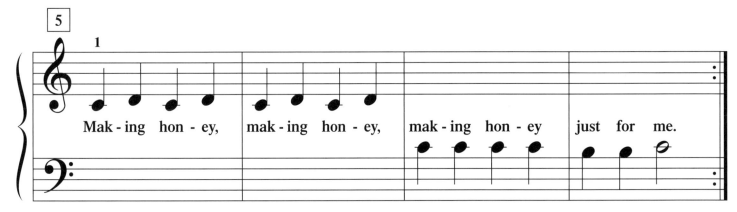

Mak - ing hon - ey, mak - ing hon - ey, mak - ing hon - ey just for me.

Teacher Duet: Student plays as written.

mf

24

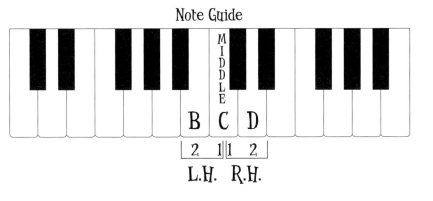

Long and Sharp 🔵11

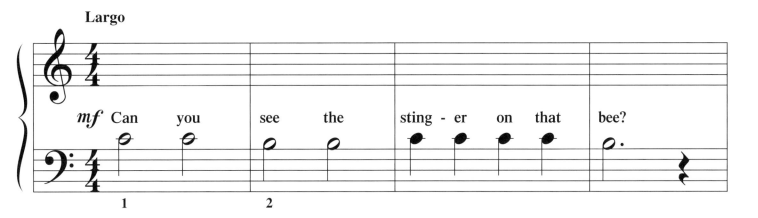

Largo

mf Can you see the sting - er on that bee?

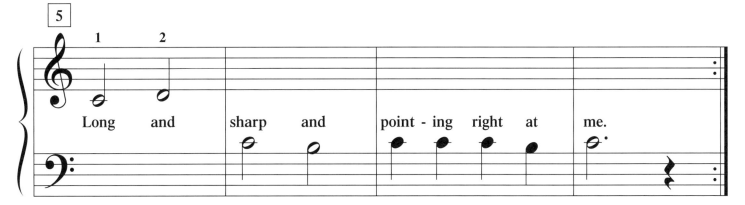

Long and sharp and point - ing right at me.

Teacher Duet: Student plays as written.

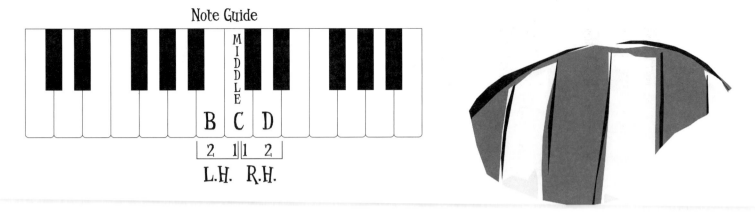

Note Guide

Yellow and Black 12

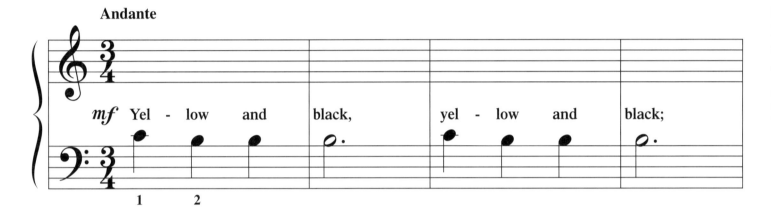

Andante

mf Yel - low and black, yel - low and black;

1   2

5

This bee is fuz - zy and yel - low and black.

1   2

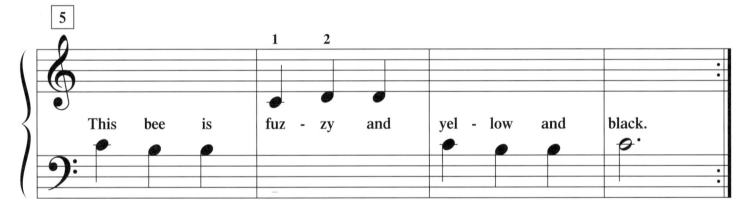

Teacher Duet: Student plays as written.

mp

5

FJH216

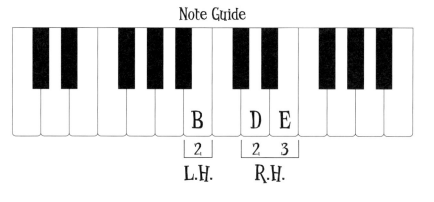

Note Guide

B 2 | D 2 E 3
L.H. | R.H.

Bumble Bee 13

Andante

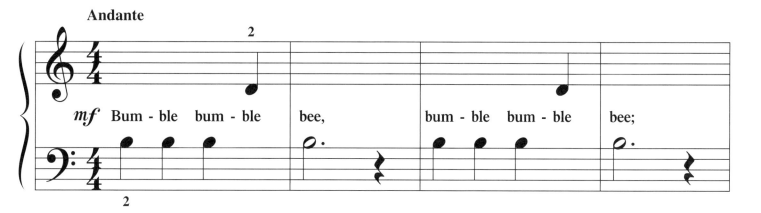

mf Bum - ble bum - ble bee, bum - ble bum - ble bee;

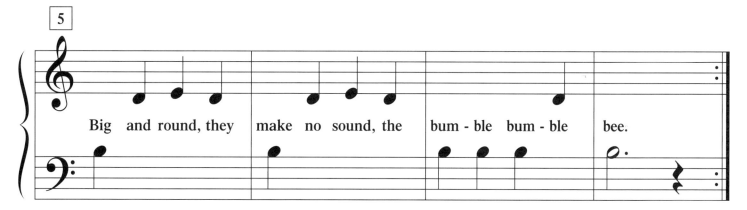

Big and round, they make no sound, the bum - ble bum - ble bee.

Teacher Duet: Student plays as written.

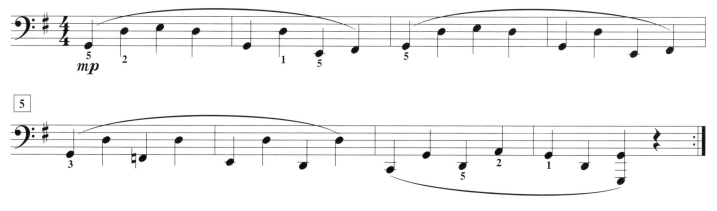

UNIT 4

Theory Made FUN Sing-Along Book tracks 1, 15-20.
Counting Made FUN Sing-Along Book tracks 21-26.
Notes Made FUN Sing-Along Book tracks 1-3, 13-15.

Alligator A

ALLIGATOR A ON THE KEYBOARD:

Find and play all of the A's on your piano. Now find the A that is below Bee Note B.
We will call it Alligator A for fun. You can play Alligator A with L.H. finger 3.

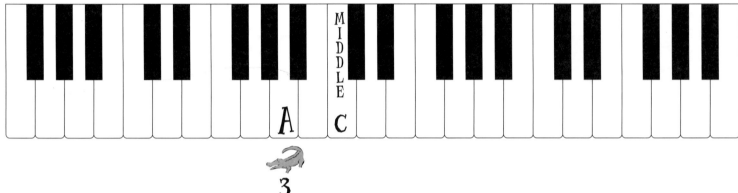

ALLIGATOR A ON THE STAFF:

Alligator A sits on line number 5 of the bass staff.

Play the example below, keeping your eyes on the music.

| 1. Name notes: | C | C | B | B | A | A | A | A | C | C | B | B | A | A | A |
| 2. Count: | 1 | 2 | 3 | 4 | 1 | 2 | 3 | 4 | 1 | 2 | 3 | 4 | 1 | 2 | 3 | 4 |

FJH216

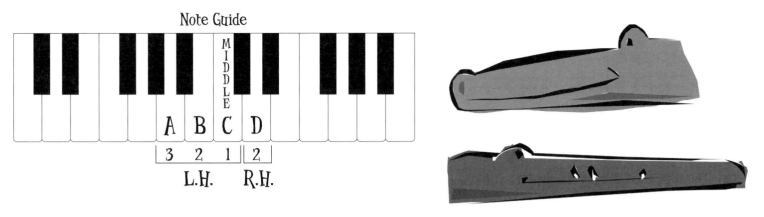

Note Guide

See You Later 14

Andante

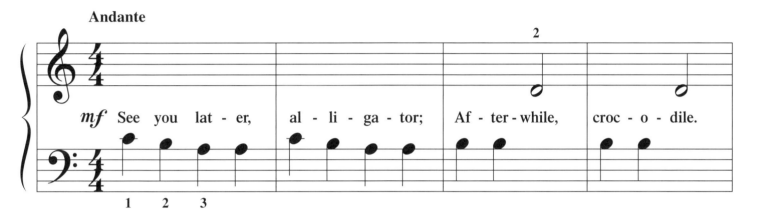

mf See you lat - er, al - li - ga - tor; Af - ter - while, croc - o - dile.

See you lat - er, al - li - ga - tor; Wave a wave and smile a smile.

Teacher Duet: Student plays as written.

mp

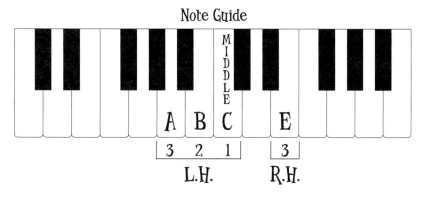

Note Guide

Angry Mood 15

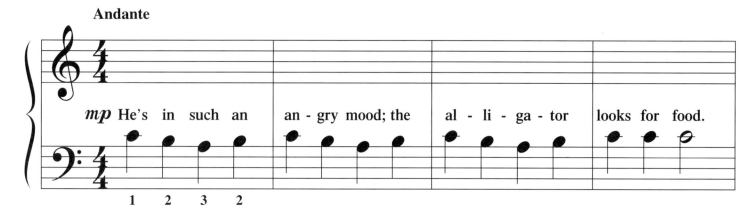

Andante

mp He's in such an an - gry mood; the al - li - ga - tor looks for food.

1 2 3 2

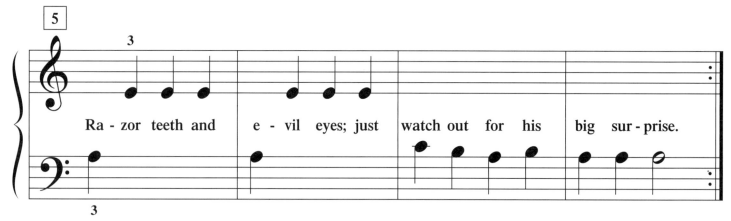

5

3

Ra - zor teeth and e - vil eyes; just watch out for his big sur - prise.

3

Teacher Duet: Student plays as written.

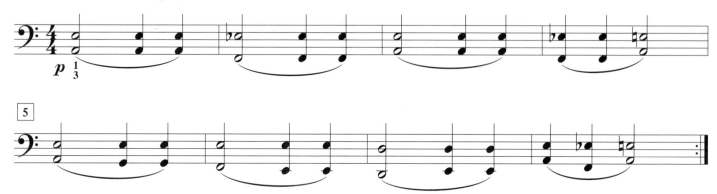

p 1
3

5

FJH2163

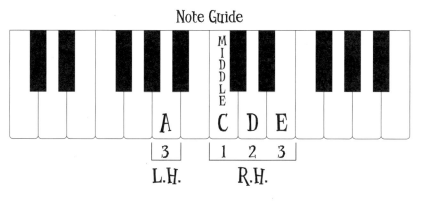

Note Guide

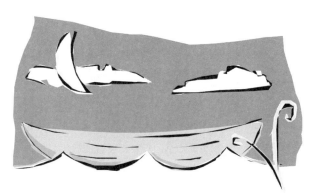

Let's Go For a Ride 16

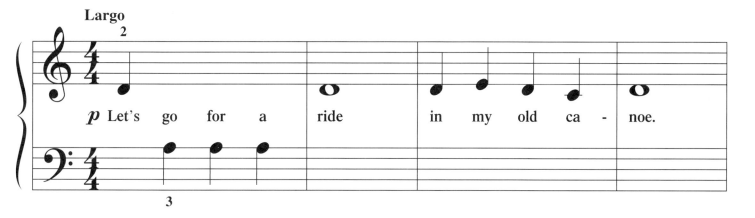

p Let's go for a ride in my old ca - noe.

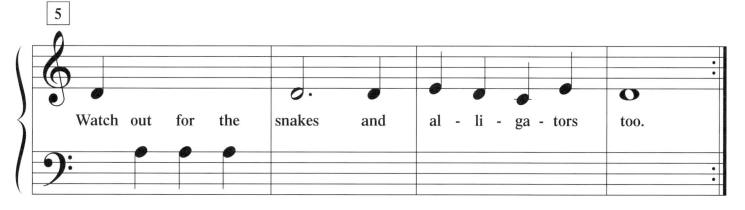

Watch out for the snakes and al - li - ga - tors too.

Teacher Duet: Student plays one octave higher.

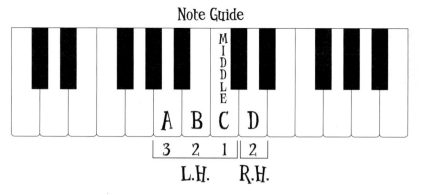

Note Guide

Bumpy and Green 17

Cat Note C to Alligator Note A is an interval of a third.

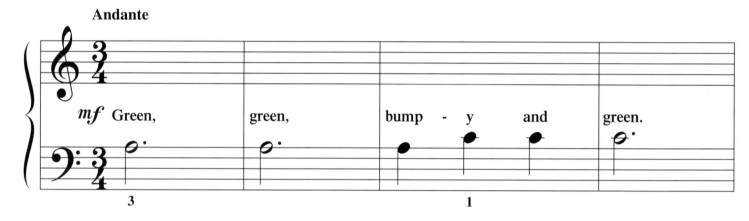

Andante

mf Green, green, bump - y and green.

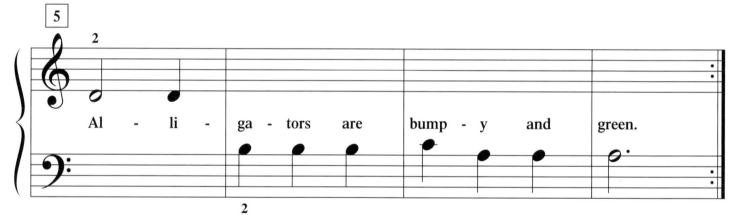

Al - li - ga - tors are bump - y and green.

Teacher Duet: Student plays as written.

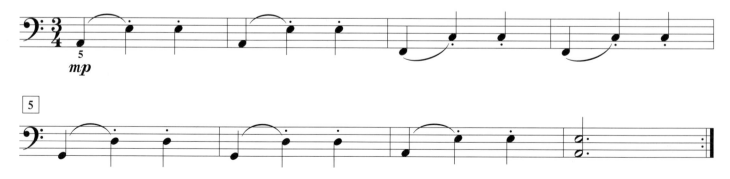

mp

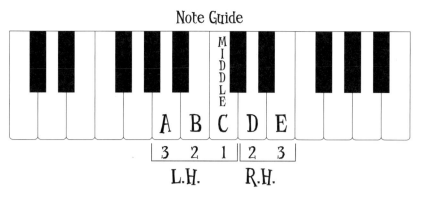

Stay Away 18

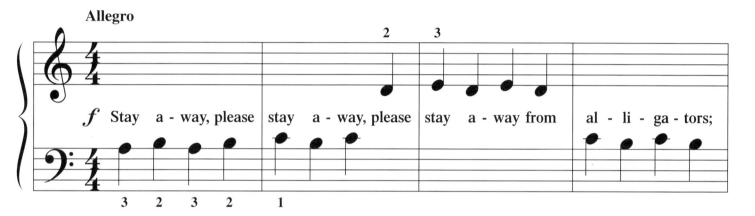

Allegro

f Stay a - way, please stay a - way, please stay a - way from al - li - ga - tors;

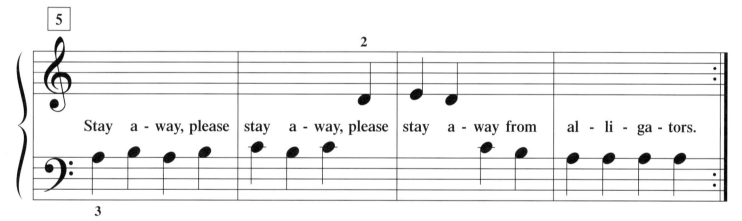

Stay a - way, please stay a - way, please stay a - way from al - li - ga - tors.

Teacher Duet: Student plays as written.

UNIT 5

Frog Note F

FROG NOTE F ON THE KEYBOARD:
Find and play all of the F's on your piano. Now find the F that is above Elephant E.
We will call it Frog Note F for fun. You can play Frog Note F with R.H. finger 4.

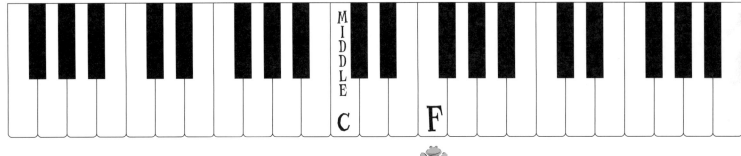

FROG NOTE F ON THE STAFF:
Frog Note F sits on space number 1 of the treble staff.

Play the example below, keeping your eyes on the music.

	1	2	3	4										
1. Name notes:	C	D	E	F	E	F	E	F	C	D	E	F	F	
2. Count:	1	2	3	4	1	2	3	4	1	2	3	4	1	2	3	4

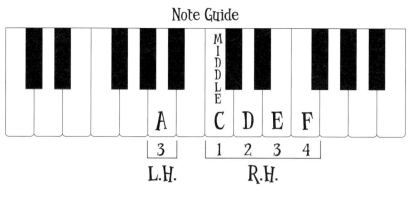

Note Guide

Moonlight on Lily Pond 19

Cat Note C to Frog Note F is an interval of a fourth.

Andante

p Moon-light shin - ing, moon-light shin - ing, on the lil - y pond.

Hold right pedal throughout the entire piece.

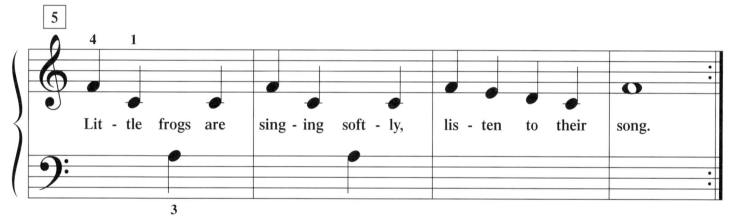

Lit - tle frogs are sing - ing soft - ly, lis - ten to their song.

Teacher Duet: Student plays one octave higher (without pedal.)

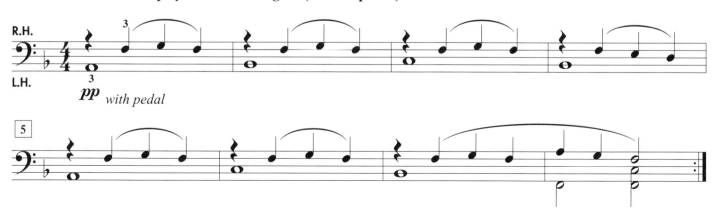

pp *with pedal*

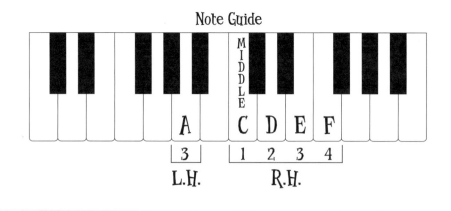

Note Guide

Hop, Hop, Hop 🔵20

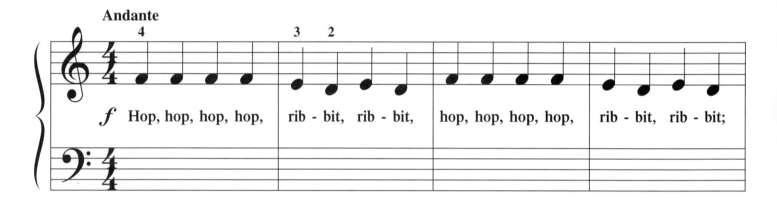

Andante

f Hop, hop, hop, hop, | rib - bit, rib - bit, | hop, hop, hop, hop, | rib - bit, rib - bit;

Watch the frog, | see him hop; | rib - bit, rib - bit, | hop, hop, hop!

Teacher Duet: Student plays one octave higher.

FJH21

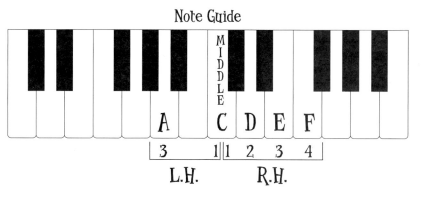

Note Guide

Slimy and Smooth 21

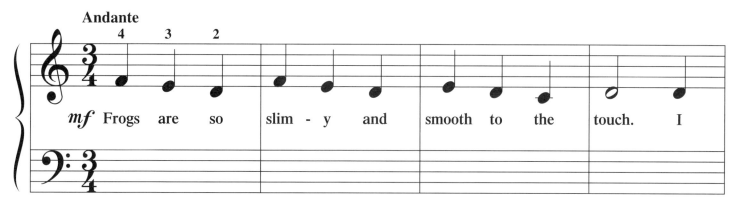

Andante

mf Frogs are so slim - y and smooth to the touch. I

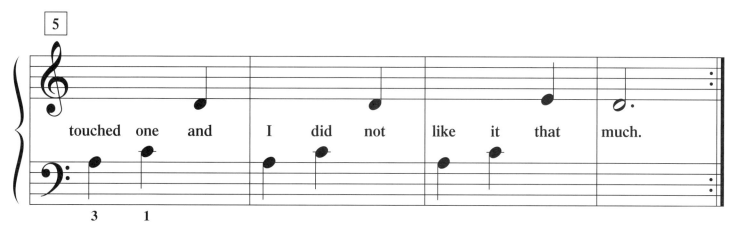

5

touched one and I did not like it that much.

Teacher Duet: Student plays one octave higher.

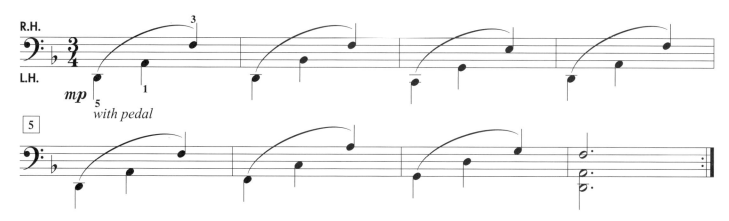

R.H.

L.H.

mp

with pedal

5

Note Guide

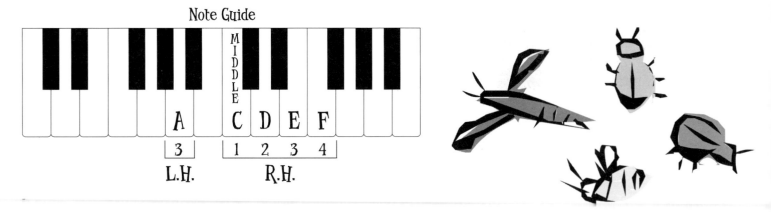

Bugs for Breakfast 22

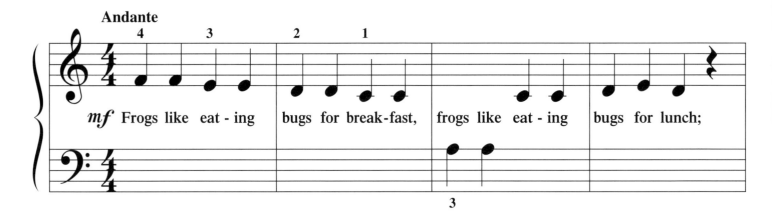

Andante

mf Frogs like eat - ing | bugs for break-fast, | frogs like eat - ing | bugs for lunch;

5

Frogs like eat - ing | bugs for din - ner; | lis - ten to the | bug - gy crunch!

Teacher Duet: Student plays as written.

mp

5

38

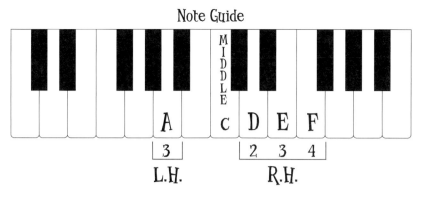

Note Guide

Tadpole ㉓

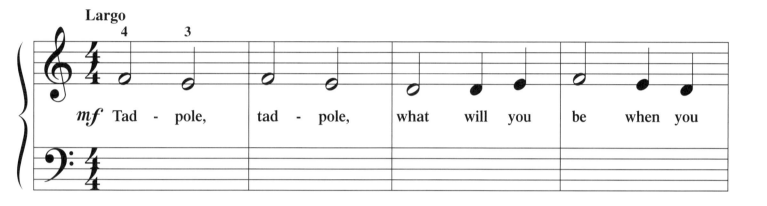

Largo

mf Tad - pole, tad - pole, what will you be when you

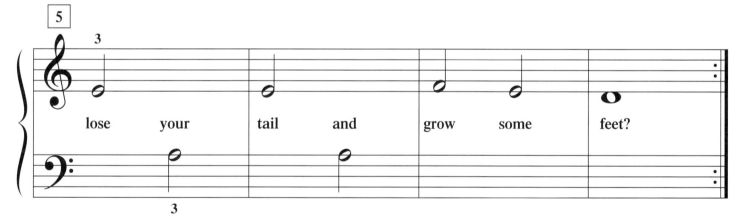

lose your tail and grow some feet?

Teacher Duet: Student plays one octave higher.

Theory Made FUN Sing-Along Book tracks 1, 15-20.
Counting Made FUN Sing-Along Book (review).
Notes Made FUN Sing-Along Book tracks 1-5, 13-15.

Giraffe Note G

GIRAFFE NOTE G ON THE KEYBOARD:
Find and play all of the G's on your piano. Now find the G that is above Frog Note F.
We will call it Giraffe Note G for fun. You can play Giraffe Note G with R.H. finger 5.

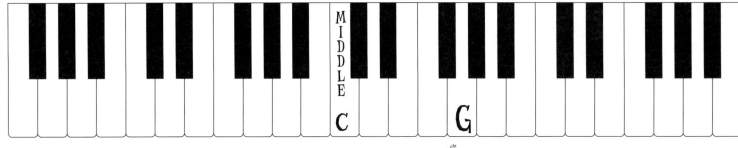

5

R.H.

GIRAFFE NOTE G ON THE STAFF:
Giraffe Note G sits on line number 2 of the treble staff.

Play the example below, keeping your eyes on the music.

| 1. Name notes: | C | D | E | F | G | G | G | | G | F | E | D | C | C | C | |
| 2. Count: | 1 | 2 | 3 | 4 | 1 | 2 | 3 | 4 | 1 | 2 | 3 | 4 | 1 | 2 | 3 | 4 |

FJH21

Note Guide

Stretch Your Neck 24

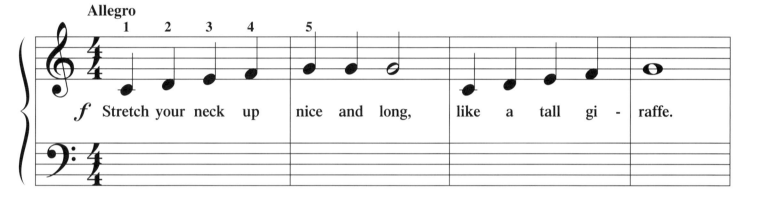

Allegro

f Stretch your neck up | nice and long, | like a tall gi - raffe.

Stretch your neck up | nice and long; | it will make you | laugh.

Teacher Duet: Student plays one octave higher.

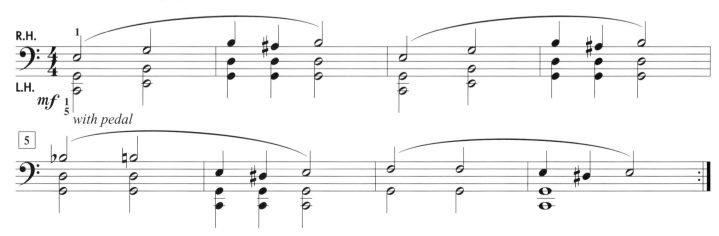

R.H.

L.H. *mf*

with pedal

JH2163

41

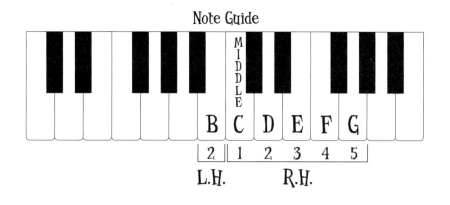

Note Guide

Africa 25

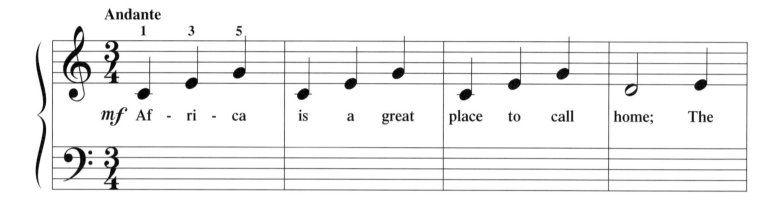

Andante

mf Af - ri - ca   is   a   great   place   to   call   home;   The

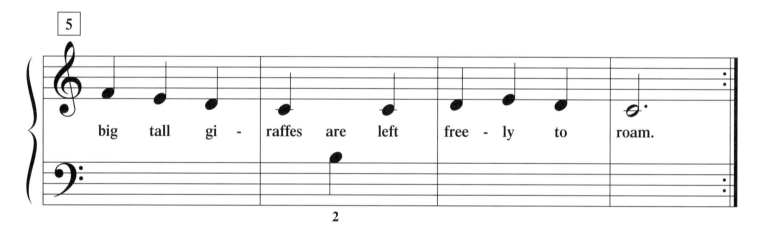

big   tall   gi - raffes   are   left   free - ly   to   roam.

Teacher Duet: Student plays one octave higher.

FJH216

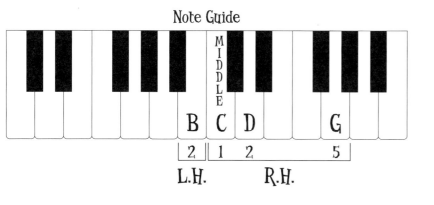

Hiding in the Trees 26

Cat Note C to Giraffe Note G is an interval of a fifth.

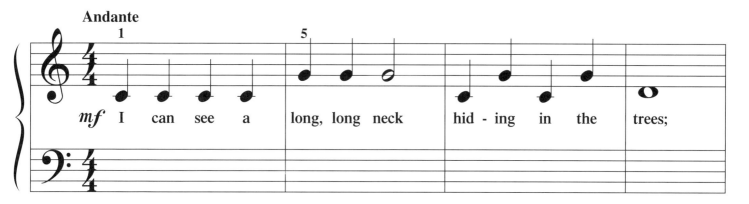

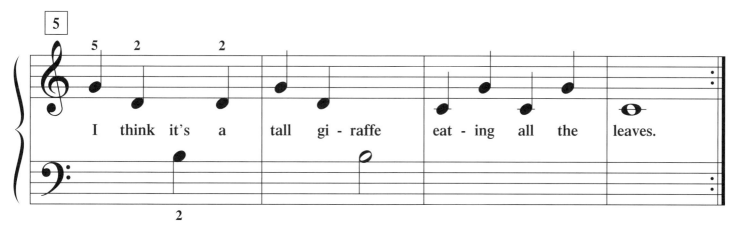

Teacher Duet: Student plays as written.

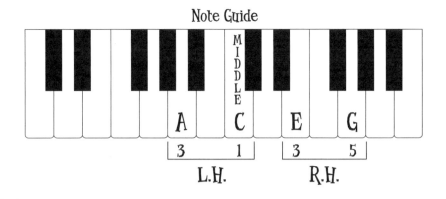

Note Guide

Yellow and Brown 27

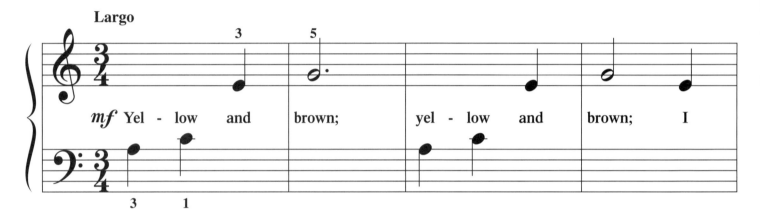

Largo

mf Yel - low and brown; yel - low and brown; I

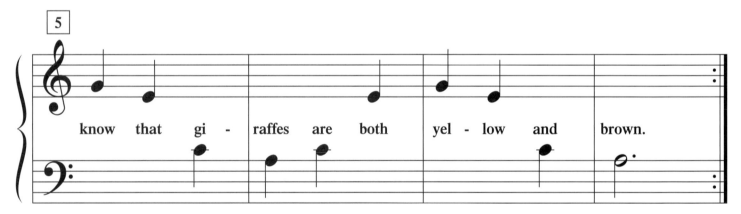

know that gi - raffes are both yel - low and brown.

Teacher Duet: Student plays one octave higher.

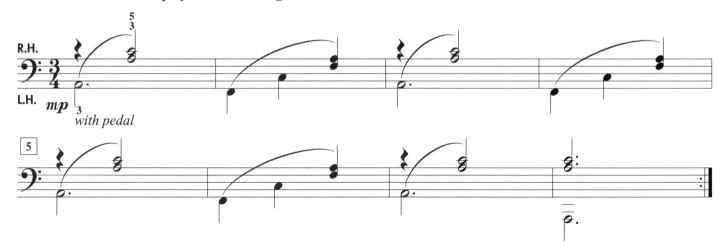

R.H.

L.H. *mp*
with pedal

FJH21

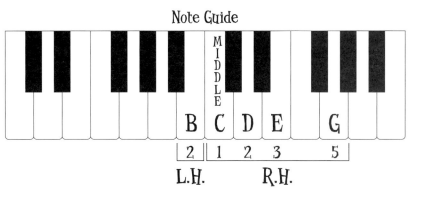

Note Guide

Let's Go See Giraffes 28

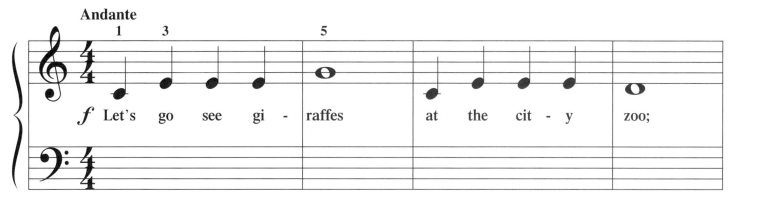

Andante

f Let's go see gi - raffes at the cit - y zoo;

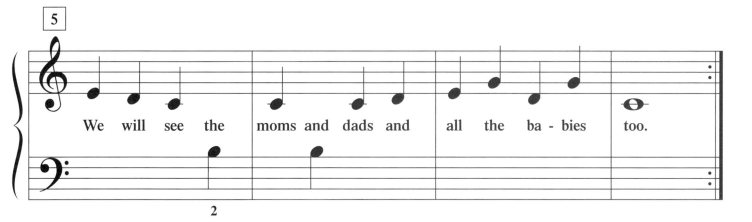

We will see the moms and dads and all the ba - bies too.

Teacher Duet: Student plays one octave higher.

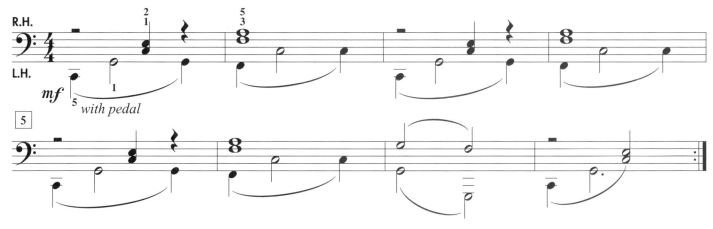

mf *with pedal*

UNIT 7

Rug Time

Theory Made FUN Sing-Along Book tracks 1, 15-20.
Counting Made FUN Sing-Along Book (review).
Notes Made FUN Sing-Along Book tracks 1-5, 13-16.

Piano Time

Gorilla Note G

GORILLA NOTE G ON THE KEYBOARD:
Find and play all of the G's on your piano. Now find the G that is below Alligator A.
We will call it Gorilla Note G for fun. You can play Gorilla Note G with L.H. finger 4.

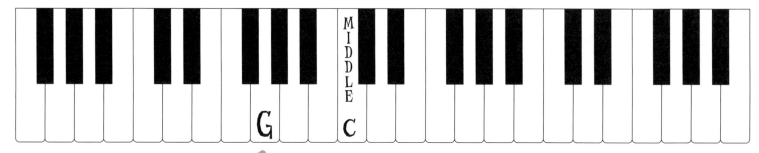

GORILLA NOTE G ON THE STAFF:
Gorilla Note G sits on space number 4 of the bass staff.

Play the example below, keeping your eyes on the music.

| 1. Name notes: C | B | A | G | A | G | A | G | C | B | A | G | A | G | C |
| 2. Count: | 1 | 2 | 3 | 4 | 1 | 2 | 3 | 4 | 1 | 2 | 3 | 4 | 1 | 2 | 3 | 4 |

1   2   3   4

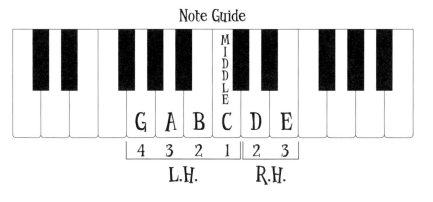

Note Guide

G A B C D E
4 3 2 1 2 3
L.H. R.H.

Brown Banana 29

Andante

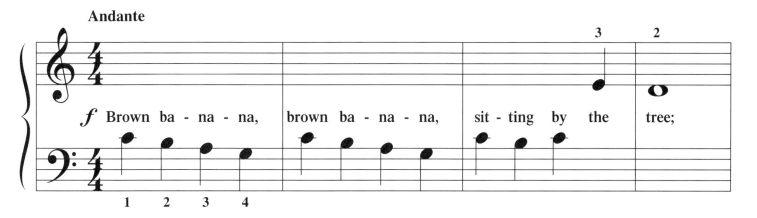

f Brown ba - na - na, brown ba - na - na, sit - ting by the tree;

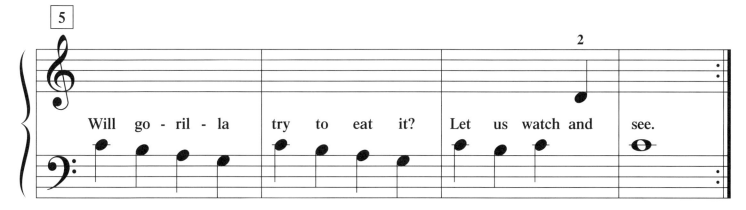

Will go - ril - la try to eat it? Let us watch and see.

Teacher Duet: Student plays one octave higher.

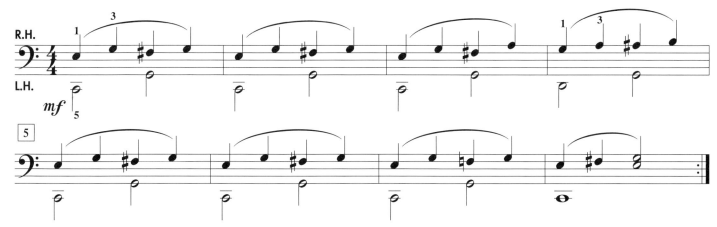

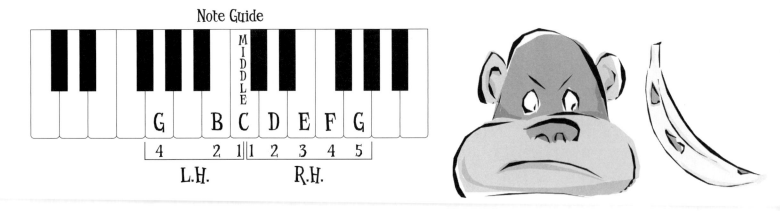

He's a Little Mad 30

Cat Note C to Gorilla Note G is an interval of a fourth.

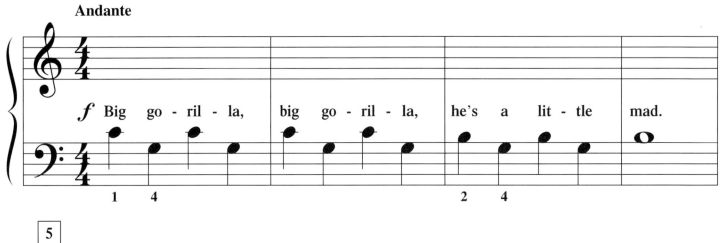

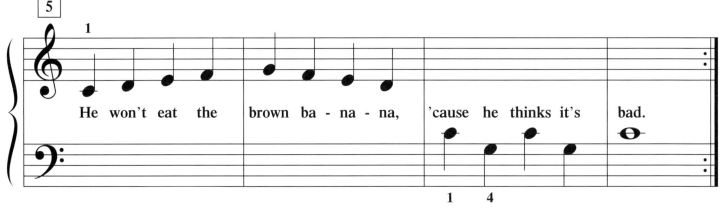

Teacher Duet: Student plays one octave higher.

48

FJH21(

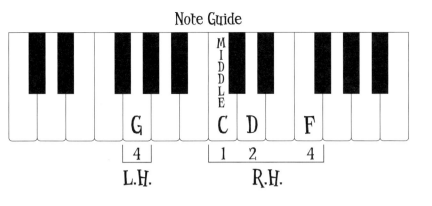

Ooh Ooh, Ah Ah 31

Allegro

Lis - ten to go - ril - la say   ooh ooh, ah ah,   ooh ooh, ah ah.

I think he just   wants to play;   Ooh ooh, ah ah,   ooh ooh, ah ah.

Teacher Duet: Student plays one octave higher.

H2163

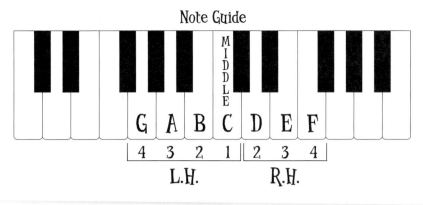

Note Guide

Watch Him Stomp 32

Andante

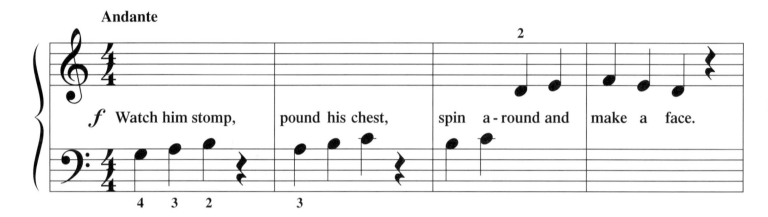

Watch him stomp, pound his chest, spin a-round and make a face.

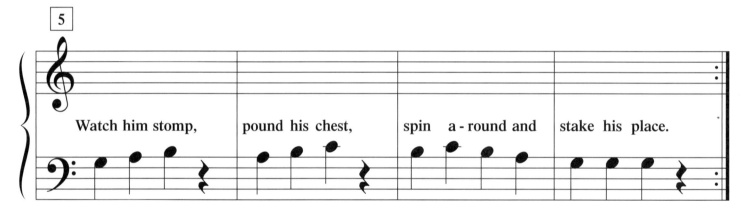

Watch him stomp, pound his chest, spin a-round and stake his place.

Teacher Duet: Student plays one octave higher.

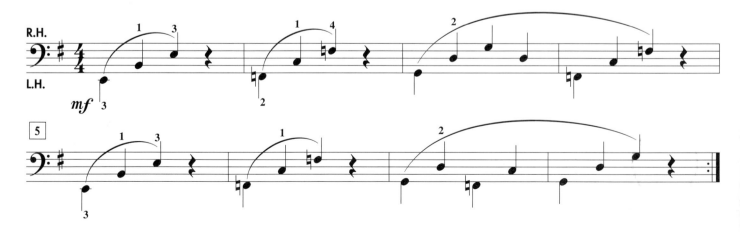

50   FJH21

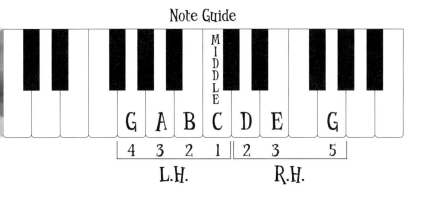

Note Guide

Nice and Soft 33

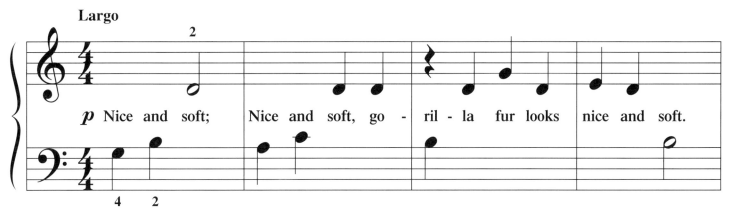

Largo

p Nice and soft; Nice and soft, go - ril - la fur looks nice and soft.

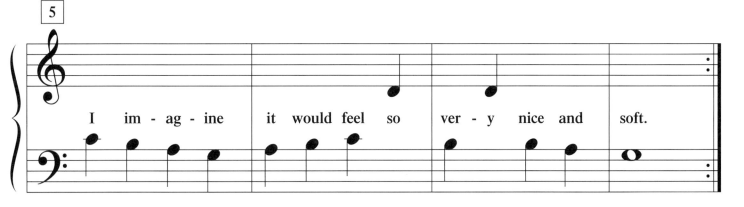

I im - ag - ine it would feel so ver - y nice and soft.

Teacher Duet: Student plays one octave higher.

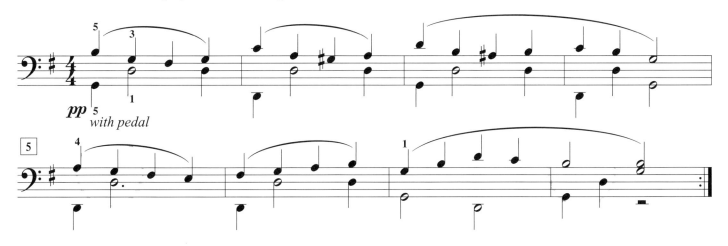

pp *with pedal*

UNIT 8

Rug Time

Theory Made FUN Sing-Along Book tracks 1, 15-20.
Counting Made FUN Sing-Along Book (review).
Notes Made FUN Sing-Along Book tracks 1-5, 13-17.

Piano Time

Fish Note F

FISH NOTE F ON THE KEYBOARD:

Find and play all of the F's on your piano. Now find the F that is below Gorilla Note G.
We will call it Fish Note F for fun. You can play Fish Note F with L.H. finger 5.

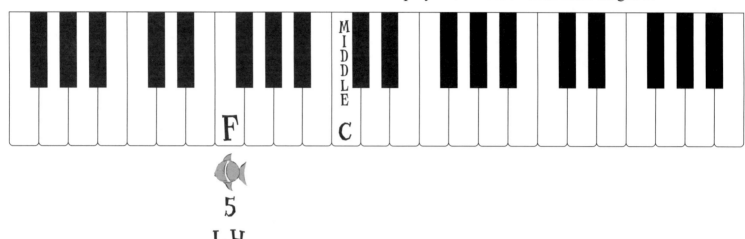

FISH NOTE F ON THE STAFF:

Fish Note F sits on line number 4 of the bass staff.

Play the example below, keeping your eyes on the music.

1. Name notes:	C	B	A	G	F	F	F		F	G	A	B	C	C	C	
2. Count:		*1*	*2*	*3*	*4*	*1*	*2*	*3*	*4*	*1*	*2*	*3*	*4*	*1*	*2*	*3*	*4*

1   2   3   4   5

52

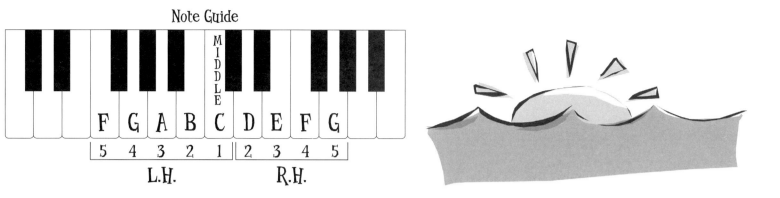

Swimming in the Ocean 🔵34

Allegro

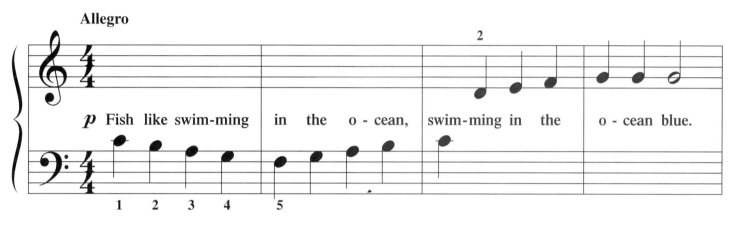

p Fish like swim-ming in the o-cean, swim-ming in the o-cean blue.

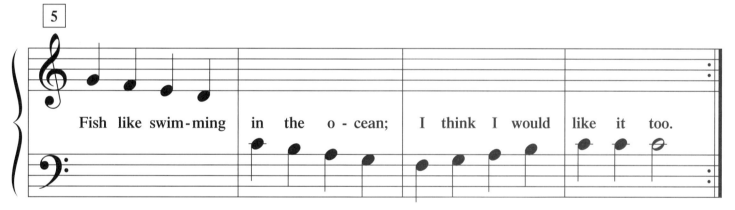

Fish like swim-ming in the o-cean; I think I would like it too.

Teacher Duet: Student plays one octave higher.

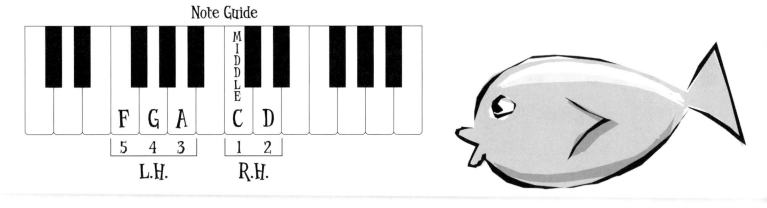

Shimmery Gold 🔘35

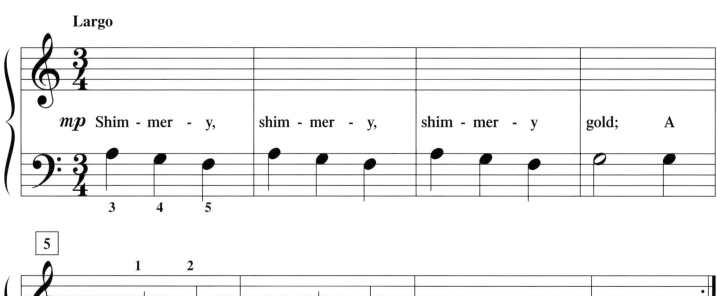

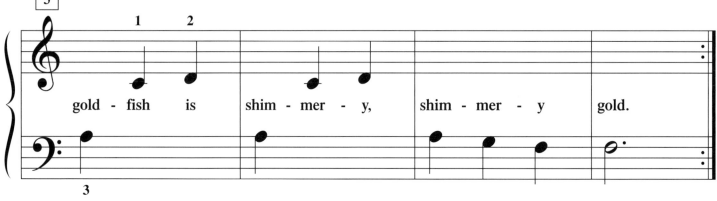

Teacher Duet: Student plays as written.

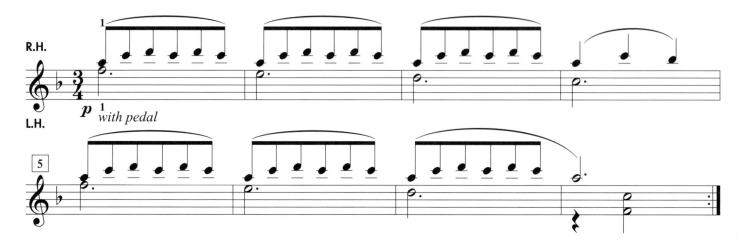

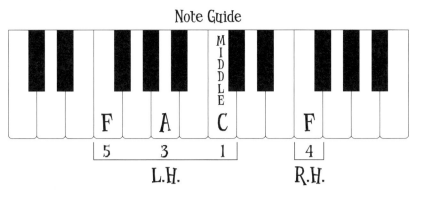

Note Guide

Smart Little Fish 36

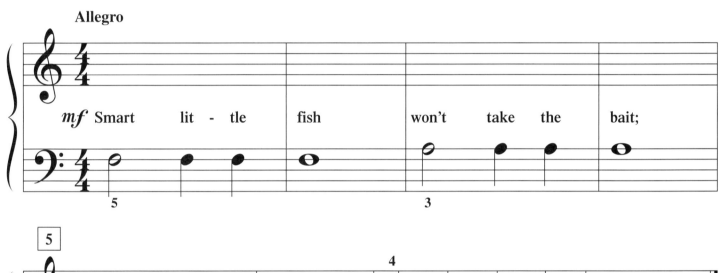

Allegro

mf Smart lit - tle fish won't take the bait;

He'd like to stay off the din - ner plate.

Teacher Duet: Student plays one octave higher.

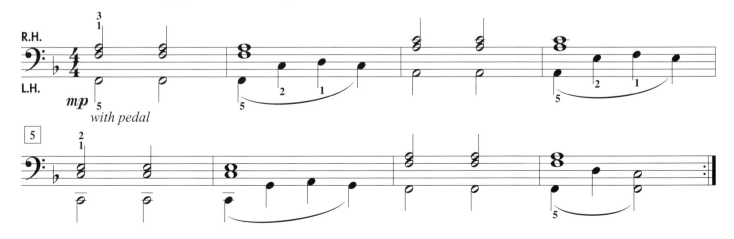

R.H.

L.H.

mp
with pedal

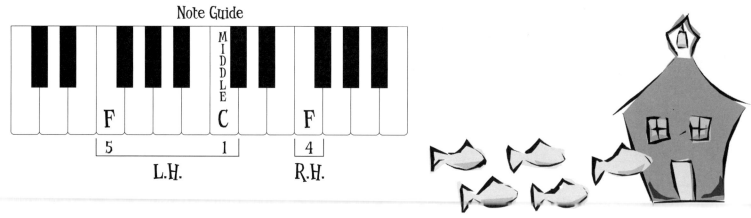

Fish Don't Go to School (37)

Cat Note C to Fish Note F is an interval of a fifth.

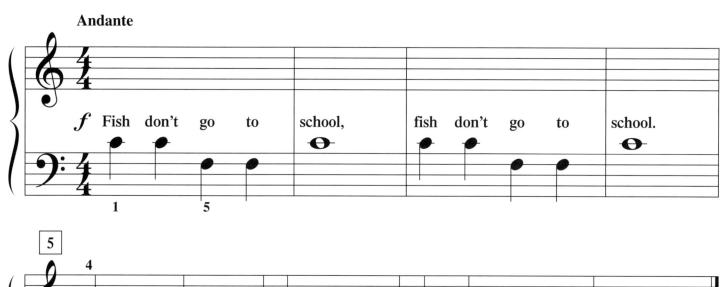

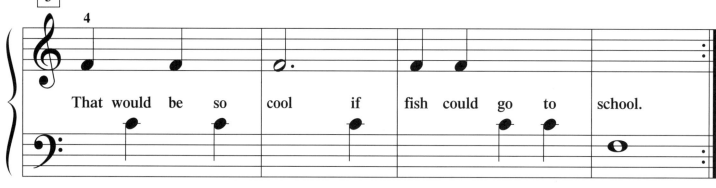

Teacher Duet: Student plays one octave higher.

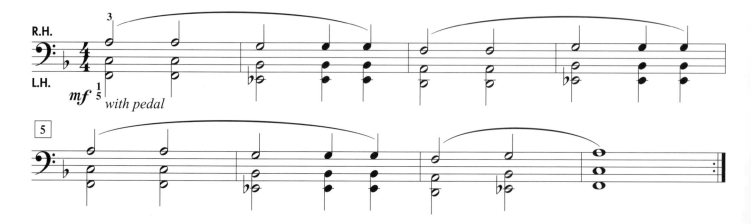

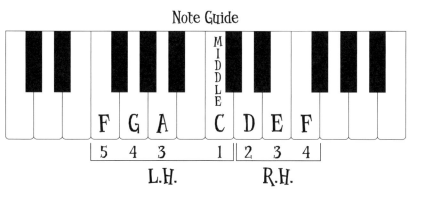

Note Guide

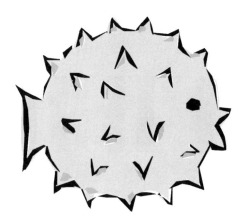

Puffer Fish 38

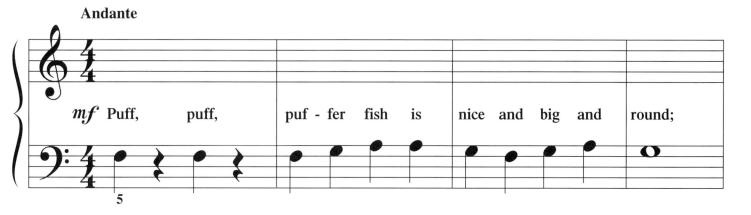

Andante

mf Puff, puff, puf - fer fish is nice and big and round;

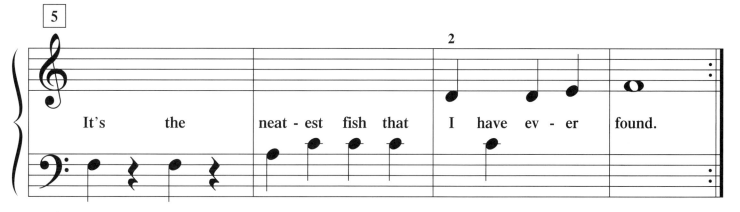

It's the neat - est fish that I have ev - er found.

Teacher Duet: Student plays as written.

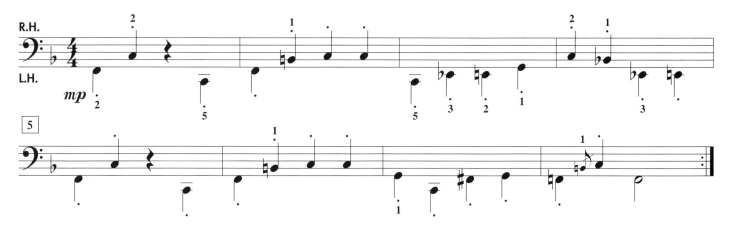

R.H.

L.H.

mp

On these pages, you could practice writing your notes, or even try writing your own songs.
You can also print more of these pages at **www.PianoMadeFun.com**.

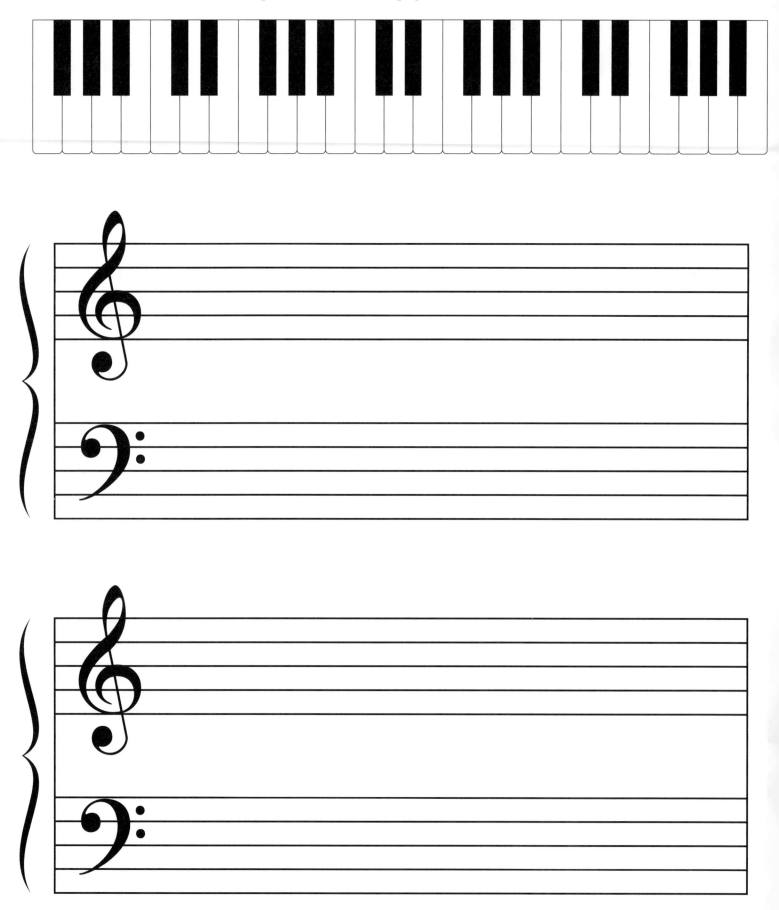

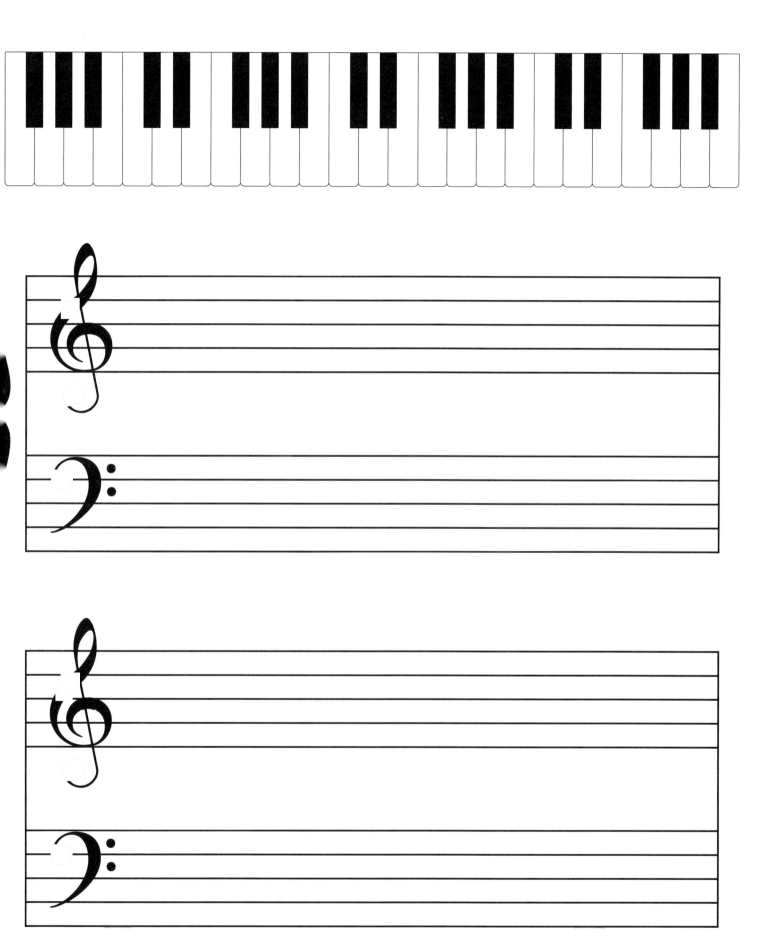

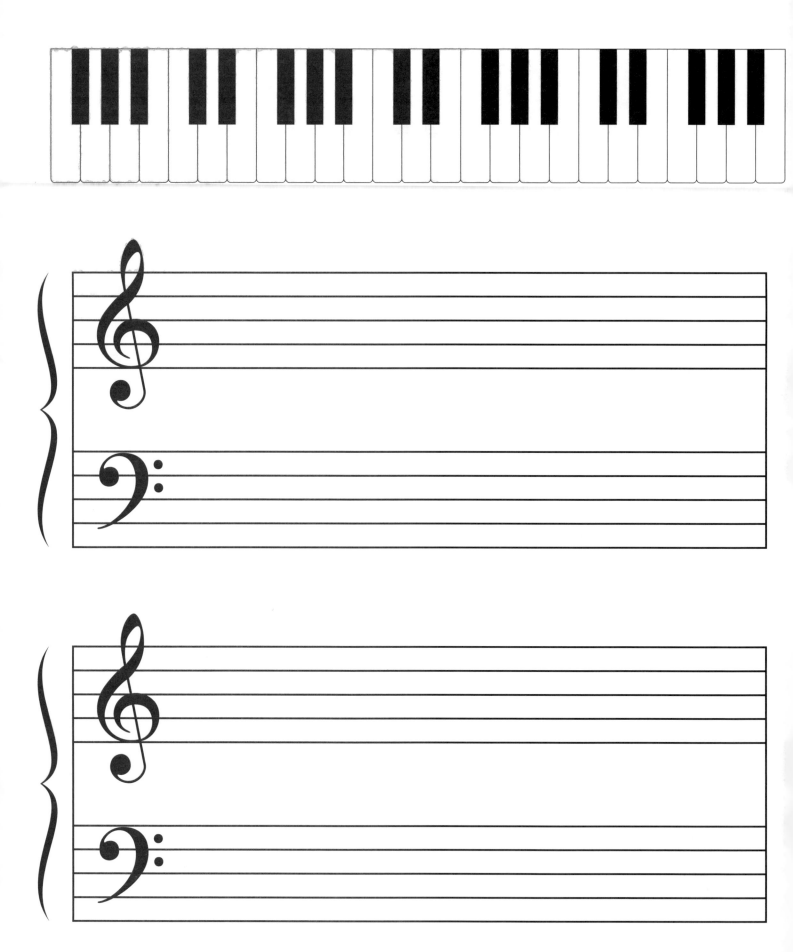

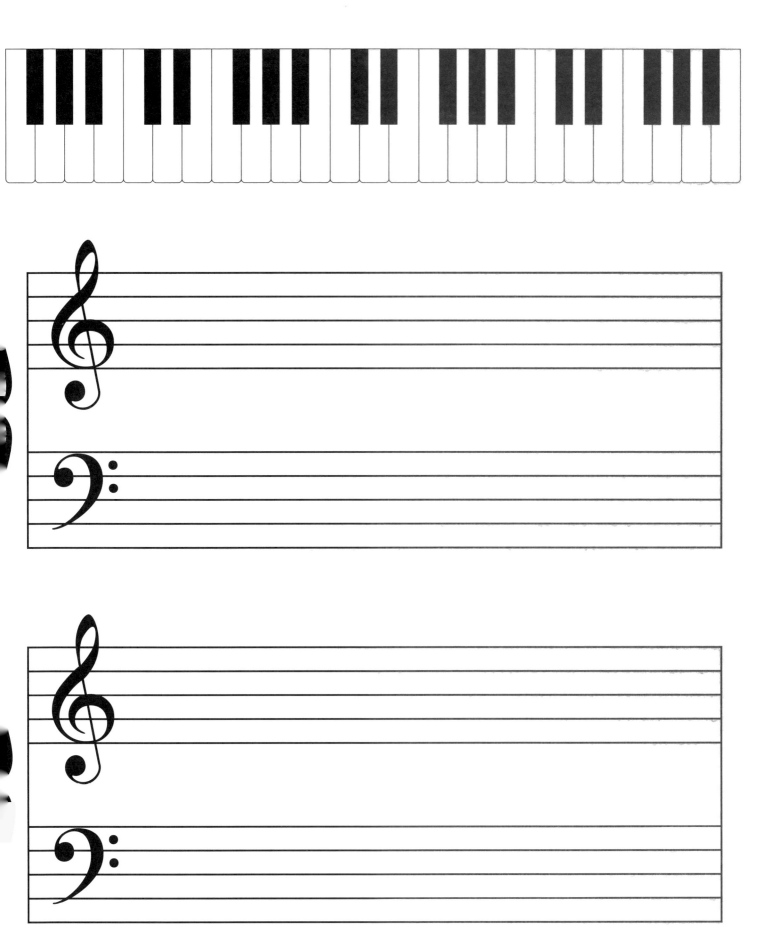

H2163

61

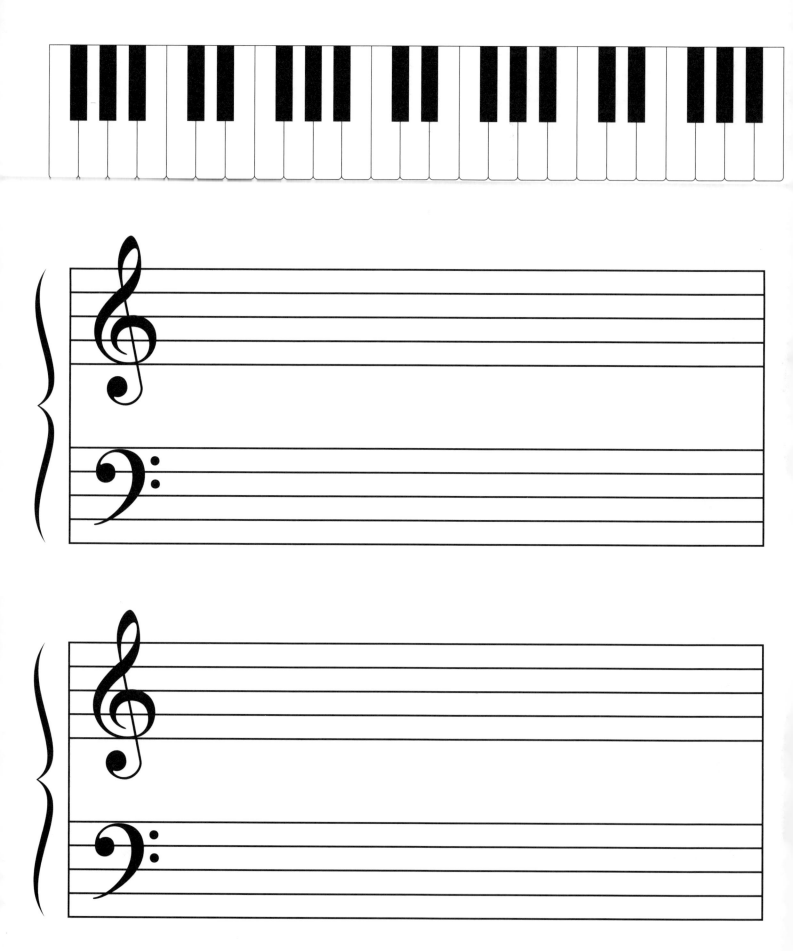

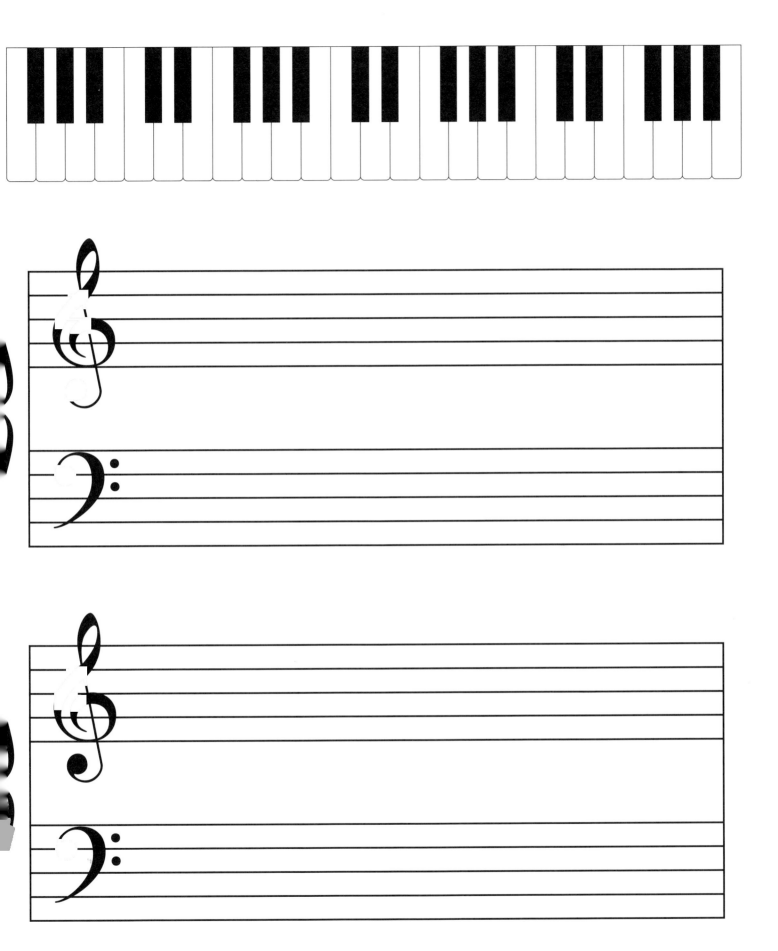

_____
Student

Congratulations!

You have now completed the

Note Reading Made FUN

Book 1

You are now ready to move on to

Note Reading Made FUN

Book 2

THE
F·J·H
MUSIC
COMPANY
I N C.
Frank J. Hackinson

_____   _____
Date   Teacher's Signature